Let's Practice Together

We have recorded all the songs in this book (see the front of this book for more details). When your teacher is not there, instead of practicing by yourself, you can play along with us. Practicing will be more fun and you will learn much quicker.

 ← This icon with a number indicates that a recorded example is available.

Practice the examples on your own, playing slowly at first. Then try playing with a metronome set to a slow tempo, until you can play the example evenly and without stopping. Gradually increase the tempo as you become more confident and then you can try playing along with the recordings.

Tuning

Before you begin each lesson or practice session you will need to tune your instrument. If it's out of tune, everything you play will sound incorrect even though you are playing the correct notes. Tuning is difficult at first, so it is best to have your teacher tune your instrument whenever possible. In time, you will be able to do it yourself easily.

 Visit our Website
www.learntoplaymusic.com

 Contact us via email
info@learntoplaymusic.com

 Like us on Facebook
www.facebook.com/LearnToPlayMusic

 Follow us on Twitter
twitter.com/LTPMusic

 View our YouTube Channel
www.youtube.com/learntoplaymusiccom

Published by
KOALA MUSIC PUBLICATIONS™

PROGRESSIVE GUITAR METHOD FOR YOUNG BEGINNERS: BOOK 2
ISBN: 978-0-947183-23-3
Order Code: 18323

COPYRIGHT CONDITIONS
No part of this product can be reproduced in any form
without the written consent of the publishers.
© 2016 LearnToPlayMusic.com
LTP LearnToPlayMusic™
RC-EEEI-M

Contents

Introduction page 4

Lesson 1 page 5
The Note E 5
Pop Goes the Weasel 5
For He's a Jolly Good Fellow 6

Lesson 2 page 7
The Note F 7
Frog Hop 7
Flying Frogs 7
How Dry I Am 8

Lesson 3 page 9
The Note G 9
Two Bar Strum Patterns 9
Little Miss Muffet 9
Mary Ann 10

Lesson 4 page 11
Eighth Note 11
How to Count Eight Notes 11
Alternate Picking 11
Pieces of Eight 11
Shave and a Haircut 12
Hot Cross Buns 12

Lesson 5 page 13
Eighth Note Strum Patterns 13
Up and Down Strum 13
Ten Little Indians 14
This Old Man 15
I'm a Little Teapot 15
Michael Finnegan 16
Shortnin' Bread 17

Lesson 6 page 18
The Dotted Quarter Note 18
Quarter Dot Rock 18
The Muffin Man 18
London Bridge 19

Lesson 7 page 20
First and Second Endings 20
Home, Sweet Home 20
Jingle Bells 21

Lesson 8 page 22
The Open D Note 22
The Farmer in the Dell 22
Brother John 23

Lesson 9 page 24
The D Chord 24
Duck for Cover 24
Big Ben 24
Eighth Note Strum Patterns in 3/4 time 25
Here We Go Round the Mulberry Bush 25

Lesson 10 page 26
The Note F Sharp (F♯) 26
Autumn's Theme 26
The Caissons Go Rolling Along 27

Notes, Chords and Rests 28

Introduction

Progressive Guitar Method for Young Beginners Books 1, 2 & 3 have been designed to introduce the younger student to the basics of Guitar playing and reading music. To maximize the student's enjoyment and interest, the **Progressive Young Beginner** series incorporates an extensive repertoire of well-known childrens' songs.

All the songs have been carefully graded into an easy-to-follow, lesson-by-lesson format, which assumes no prior knowledge of music or the guitar by the student. Chord symbols and easy strumming patterns are provided above each song.

Book 2 extends the range of notes to cover more than one octave, involving five new notes (E, F, G, open D and F♯), and five simplified chord shapes (G, D7 C, G7 and D). It contains very easy arrangements of over 20 songs, and introduces the student to eighth notes, eighth note strum patterns and dotted quarter notes. New pieces of information are highlighted by color boxes, and color illustrations are used throughout to stimulate and maintain the students' interest.

Progressive Guitar Method for Young Beginners - Supplementary Songbook A contains 29 extra songs to provide a repertoire to go with all the notes, terms and techniques learned in Progressive Guitar Method for Young Beginners Book 2.

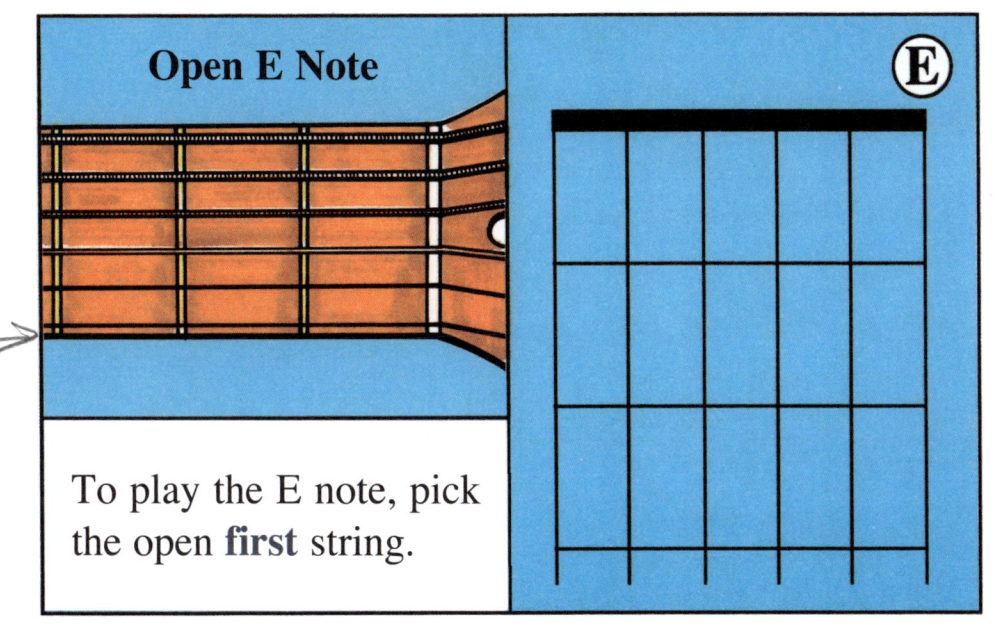

Open E Note

To play the E note, pick the open **first** string.

Lesson 1
The Note E

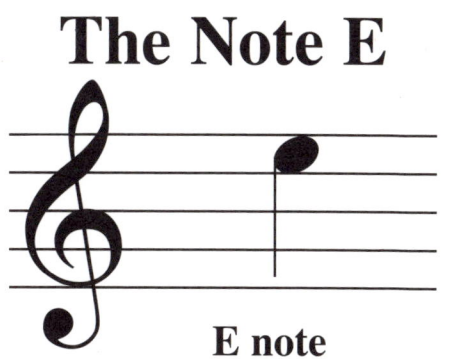

E note

This is an **E** note. The note E is written in the **fourth** space of the staff.

 **1 Pop Goes the Weasel**

To play the rests in bar **13**, stop the E note from sounding by lightly touching it with the **first** finger of your left hand.

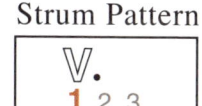

Strum Pattern

Half a pound of tup - pe - ny rice, half a pound of trea - cle,
mix them up and make ___ it nice, Pop! goes the wea - sel.

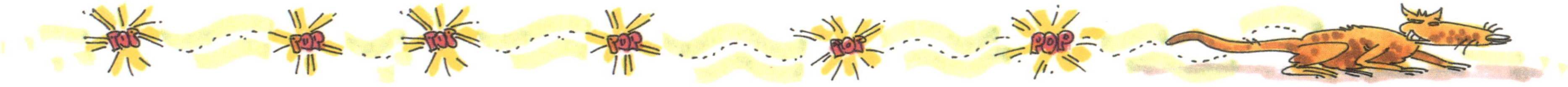

 **2 For He's a Jolly Good Fellow**

On the recording there are **five** drumbeats to introduce this song.

D.C. al Fine (pronounced "fee-nay")

The instruction ***D.C. al Fine*** is written over bar **24**. This means that you play the song again from the beginning until you reach the word ***Fine***.

Strum Pattern

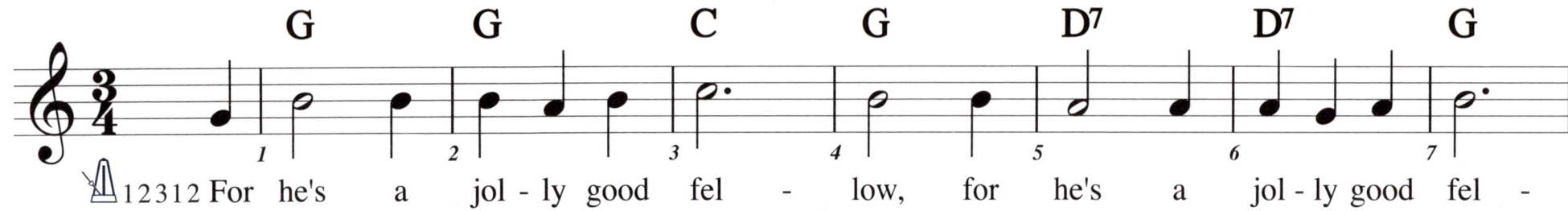

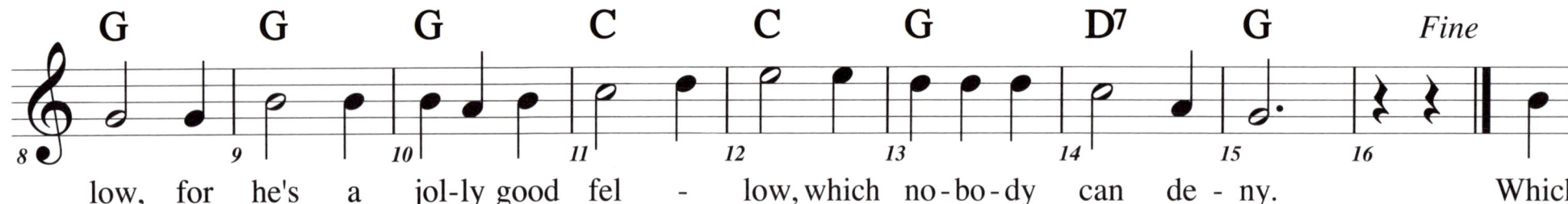

You can now play the songs on pages 5 to 9 of Guitar Method for Young Beginners, Supplementary Songbook A.

 **5 How Dry I Am**

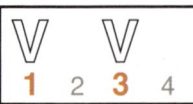
Strum Pattern

On the recording there are **five** drumbeats to introduce this song.

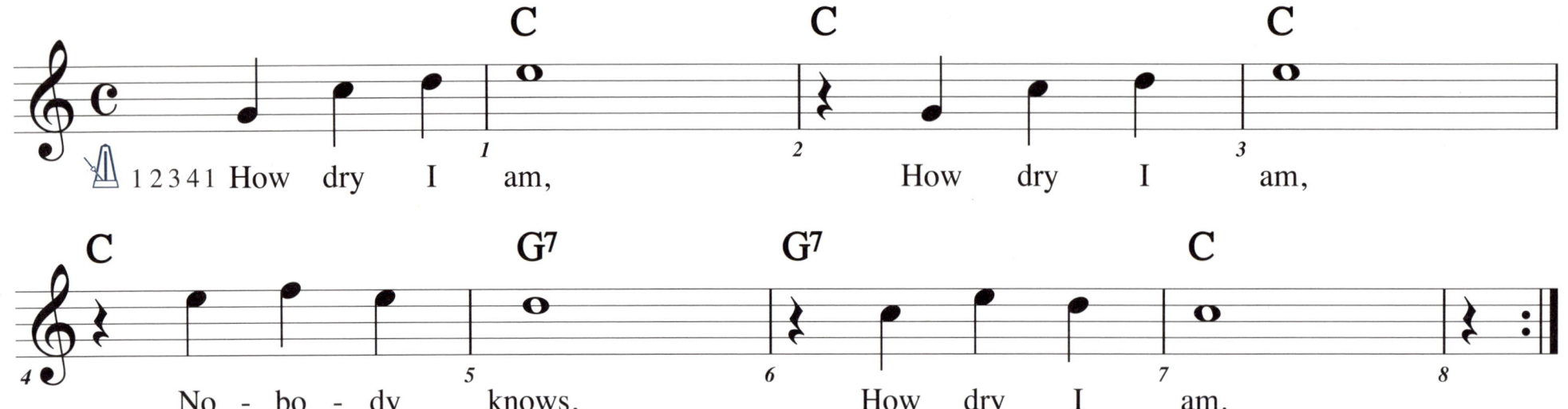

1 2 3 4 1 How dry I am, / How dry I am, / No-bo-dy knows, / How dry I am.

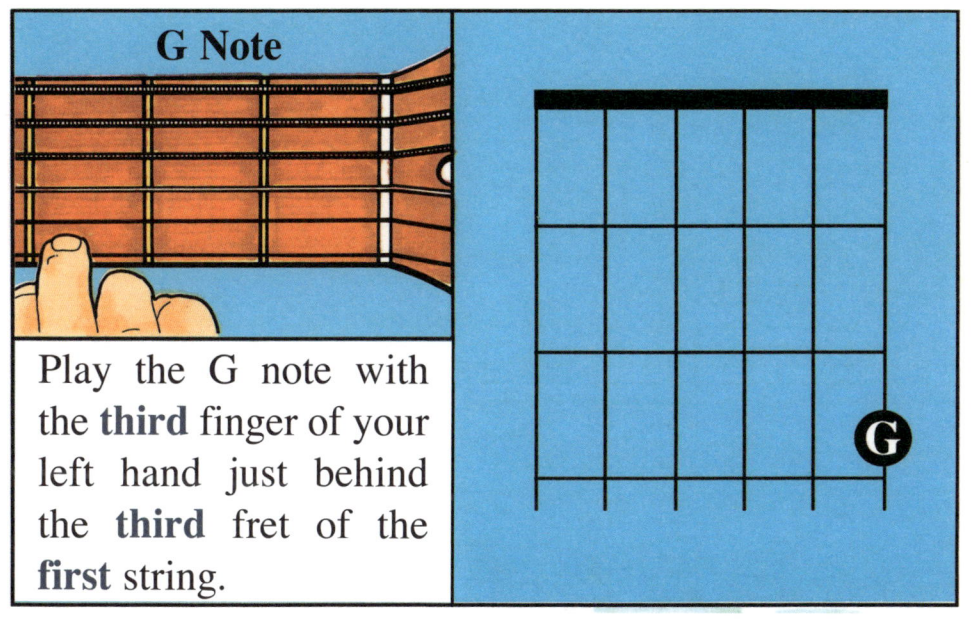

Lesson 3

The Note G

G Note

Play the G note with the **third** finger of your left hand just behind the **third** fret of the **first** string.

G

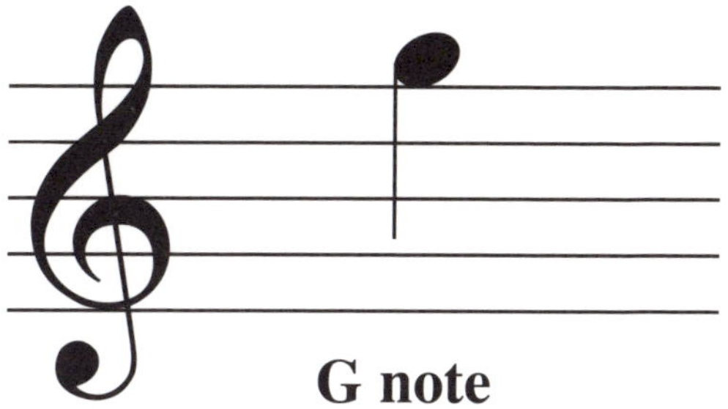

G note

This is a **G** note. The note G is written in the space **above** the staff.

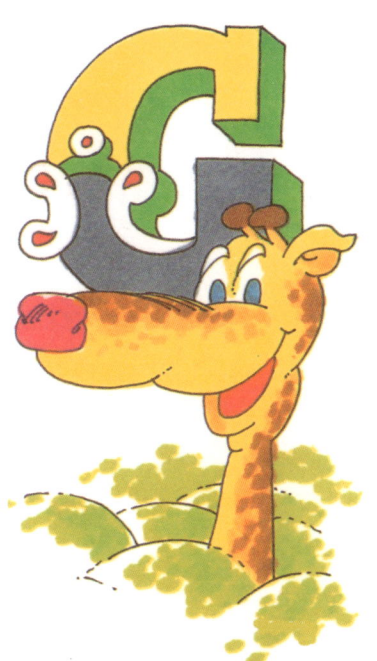

Two Bar Strum Patterns

So far all the strum patterns you have were **one bar long**. In the song **Little Miss Muffet**, use the following strum pattern which lasts for **two bars**.

Strum Pattern

Bar 1	Bar 2
V V V 1 2 3	V. 1 • 2 3

6 Little Miss Muffet

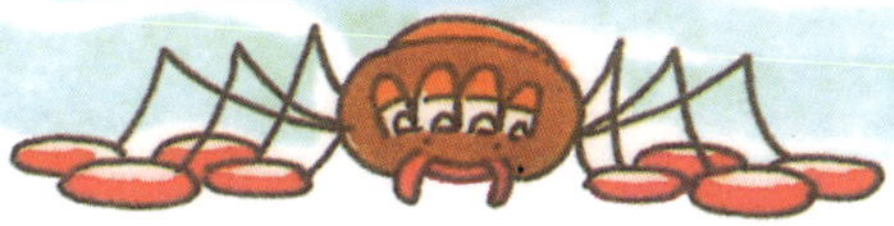

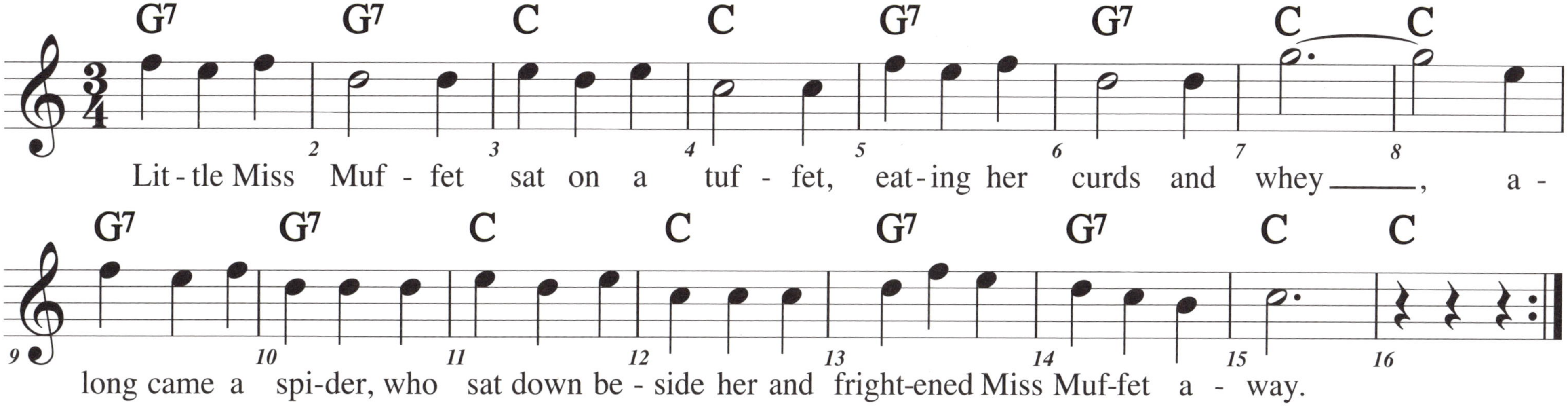

G7 G7 C C G7 G7 C C
Lit - tle Miss Muf - fet sat on a tuf - fet, eat - ing her curds and whey ___, a -
G7 G7 C C G7 G7 C C
long came a spi - der, who sat down be - side her and fright - ened Miss Muf - fet a - way.

Lesson 4

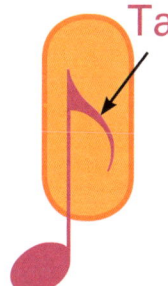

Eighth Note

This is an **eighth note**, sometimes called a quaver. It lasts for **half** a count. There are **eight** eighth notes in one bar of $\frac{4}{4}$ time.

When eighth notes are joined together, the tails are replaced by one **beam**.

Two eighth notes joined together.

Four eighth notes joined together.

 **8 How to Count Eighth Notes**

Alternate Picking

All of the songs you have played so far involved a downward pick motion, indicated by V. With the introduction of eighth notes, down (V) and up (Λ) picking is used. This is called **alternate picking**. In alternate picking, use a down pick **ON** the beat (the number count) and an up pick **OFF** the beat (the 'and' count).
Try the following exercise:

9 Pieces of Eight

 **10 Shave and a Haircut**

Use alternate picking on the **second** beat of the first bar. To achieve the rest on the first beat of bar **2**, stop the third string from sounding by lightly touching it with your second finger.

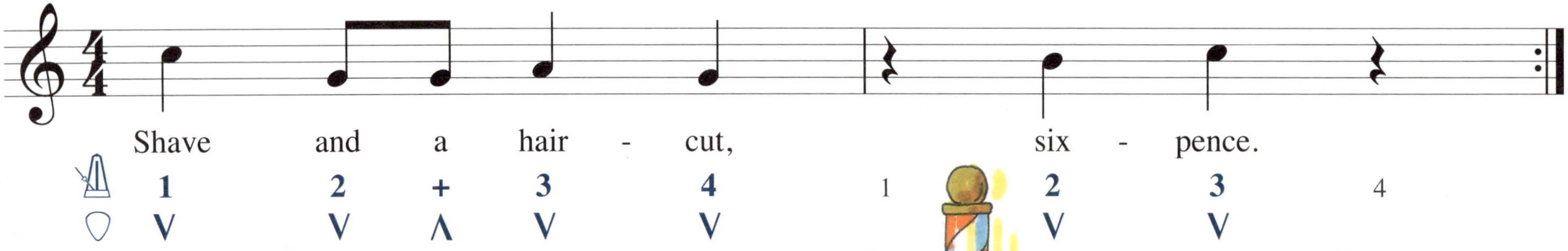

Shave — and — a — hair - cut, — six - pence.

1   2 + 3   4   1   2   3   4
V   V ∧ V   V   V   V

11 Hot Cross Buns

Strum Pattern: V V V   1 2 3 4

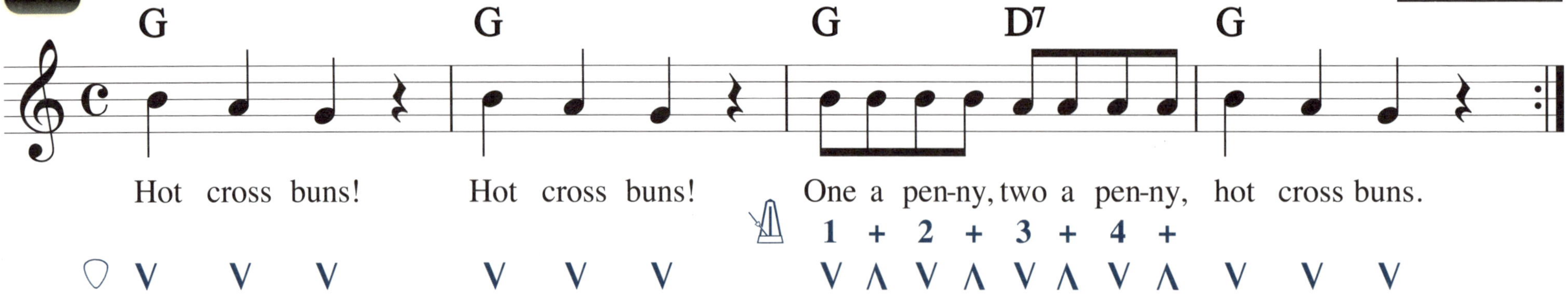

G — G — G — D⁷ — G

Hot cross buns!   Hot cross buns!   One a pen-ny, two a pen-ny, hot cross buns.

1 + 2 + 3 + 4 +
V V V V V V V∧V∧V∧V∧ V V V

You can now play the songs on pages 12 to 14 of Guitar Method for Young Beginners, Supplementary Songbook A.

Lesson 5

Eighth Note Strum Patterns

All the strumming patterns you have played so far involved playing a downward strum (V) on the first, second, third or fourth count. To make strumming more interesting, **eighth note** strum patterns can be used. An eighth note strum pattern uses a down and up strum within one count. An up strum is indicated by a ∧, and is played on the 'and' section of the count.

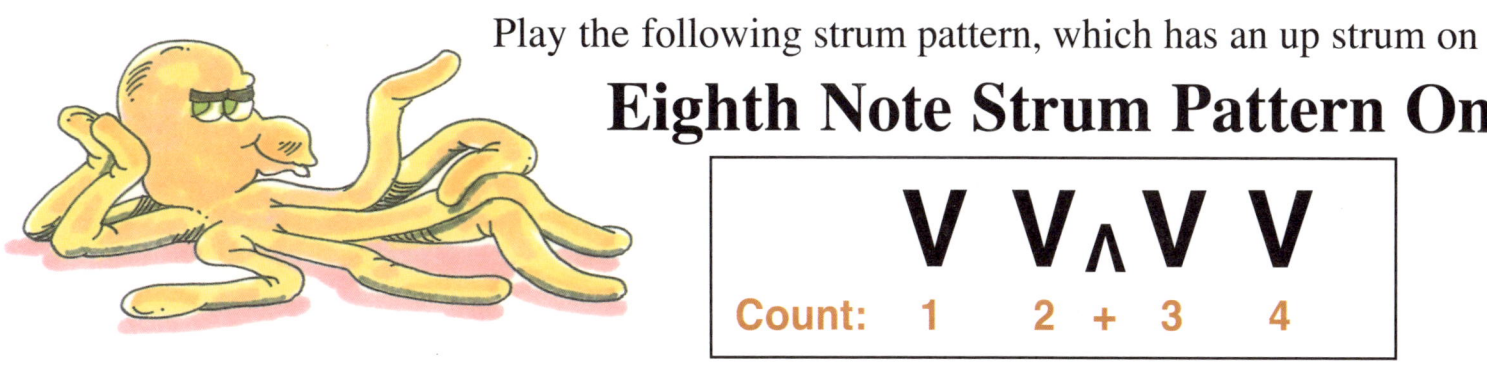

Play the following strum pattern, which has an up strum on the **second** beat.

Eighth Note Strum Pattern One

V	V∧	V	V
Count: 1	2 +	3	4

Practice this new strumming pattern holding a G chord. Hold your pick lightly and strum evenly. When strumming, only move your wrist up and down. Do not move your arm. Play the following song using **Eighth Note Strum Pattern Number One**.

12 Up and Down Strum

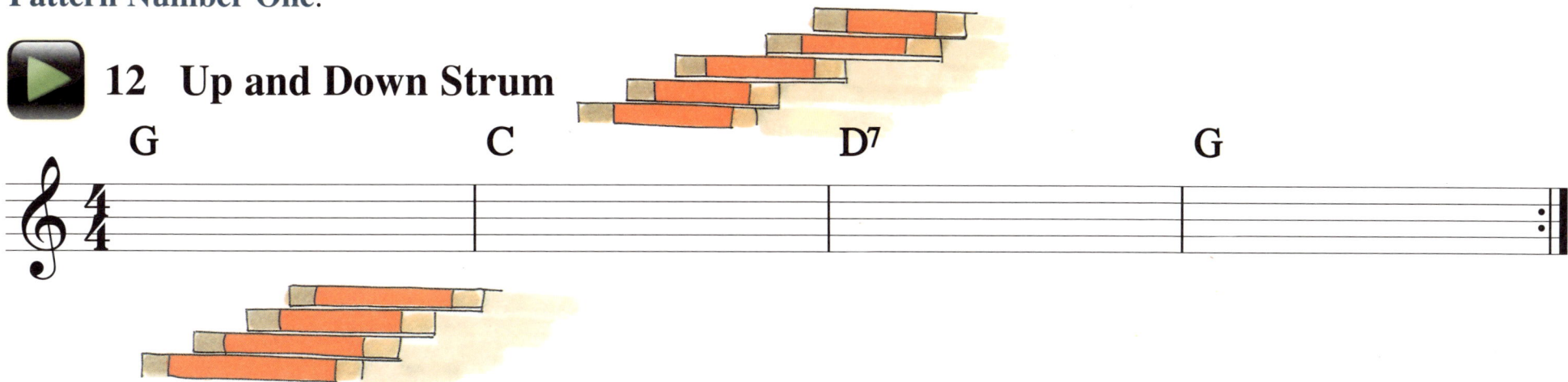

Use **Eighth Note Strum Pattern One** when playing the chords of **Ten Little Indians**.

 **13 Ten Little Indians**

| C | C | G7 | G7 |

One lit-tle two lit-tle three lit-tle In-di-ans, four lit-tle five lit-tle six lit-tle In-di-ans,

| C | C | G7 | C |

seven lit-tle eight lit-tle nine lit-tle In-di-ans, ten lit-tle In-di-an boys.

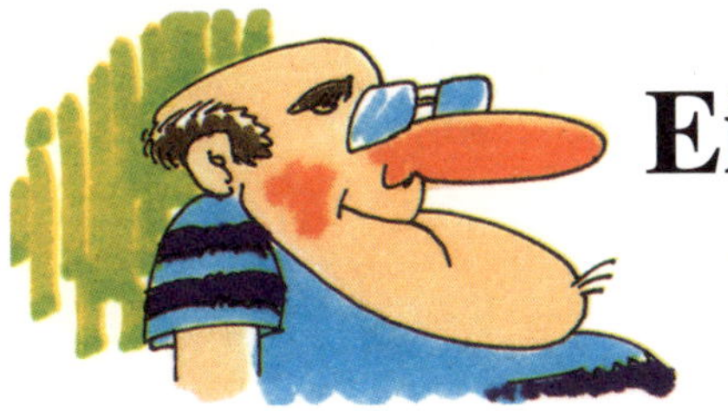

Eighth Note Strum Pattern Two

V V V∧V
Count: 1 2 3 + 4

Practice playing **Eighth Note Strum Pattern Two** holding a G chord.

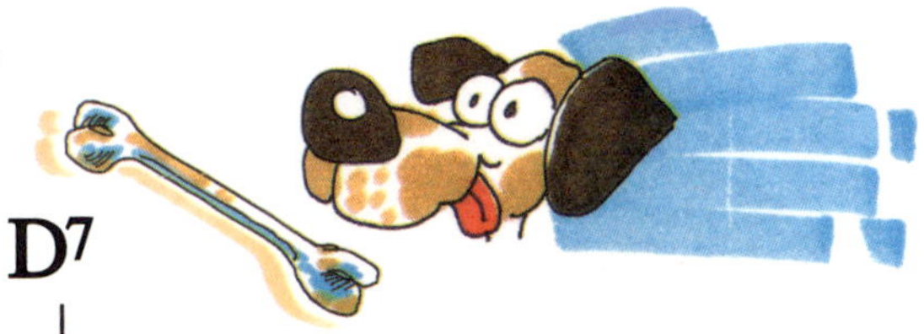

14 This Old Man

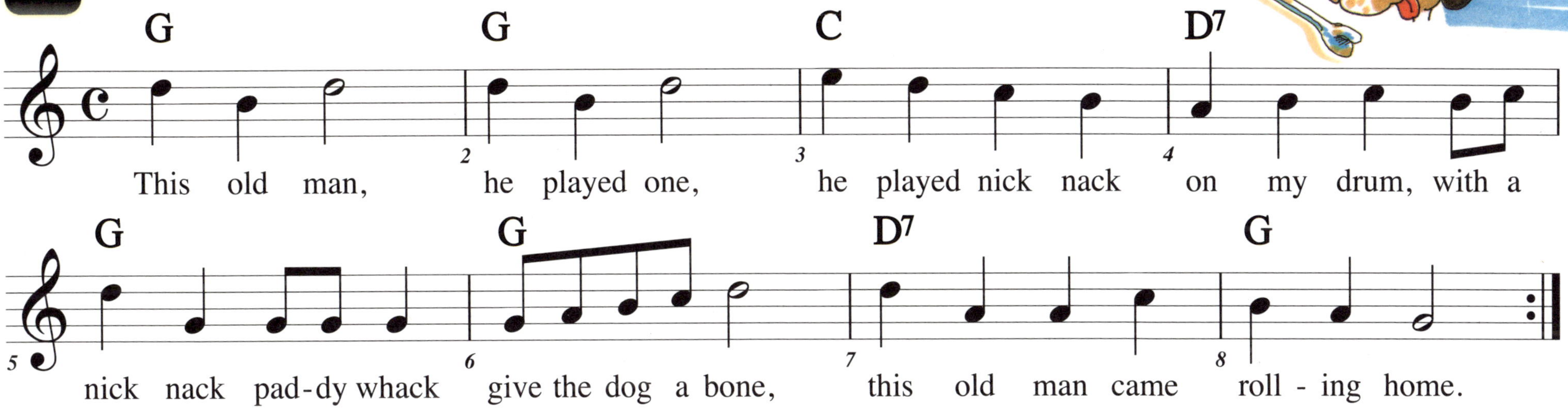

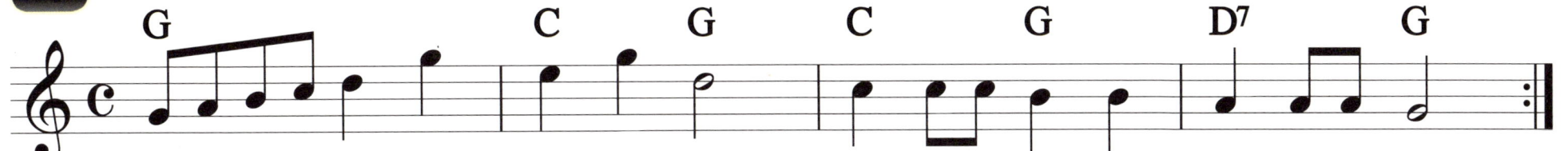

This old man, he played one, he played nick nack on my drum, with a nick nack pad-dy whack give the dog a bone, this old man came roll-ing home.

Eighth Note Strum Pattern Three

Use **Eighth Note Strum Pattern Three** in the next song.

V∧V V V
Count: 1 + 2 3 4

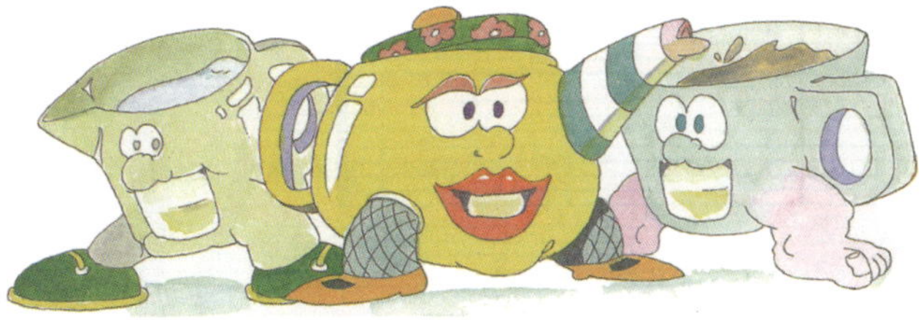

15 I'm a Little Teapot

I'm a lit-tle tea-pot, short and stout, here is my han-dle, here is my spout.

Eighth Note Strum Pattern Four

V	∧	V	∧	V	V

Count: 1 + 2 + 3 4

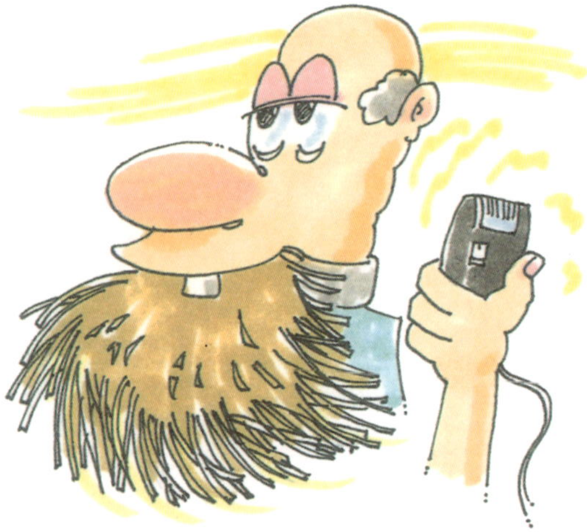

Use **Eighth Note Strum Pattern Four** in the song of **Michael Finnegan**.

16 Michael Finnegan

On the recording there are **four** drumbeats to introduce to this song.

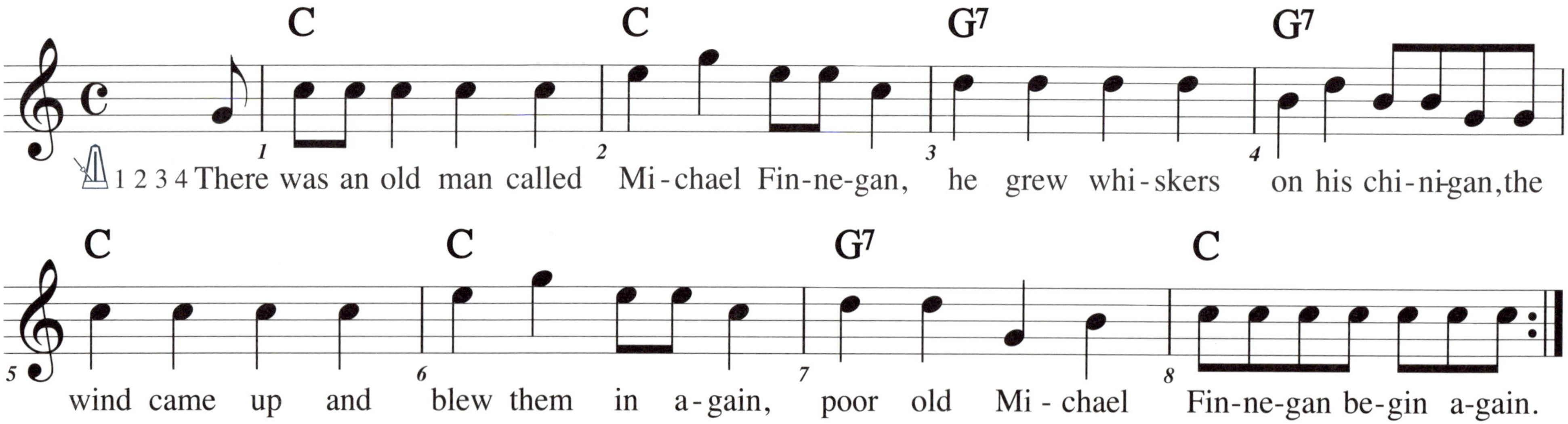
C C G7 G7
1 2 3 4 There was an old man called Mi-chael Fin-ne-gan, he grew whi-skers on his chi-ni-gan, the
C C G7 C
wind came up and blew them in a-gain, poor old Mi - chael Fin-ne-gan be-gin a-gain.

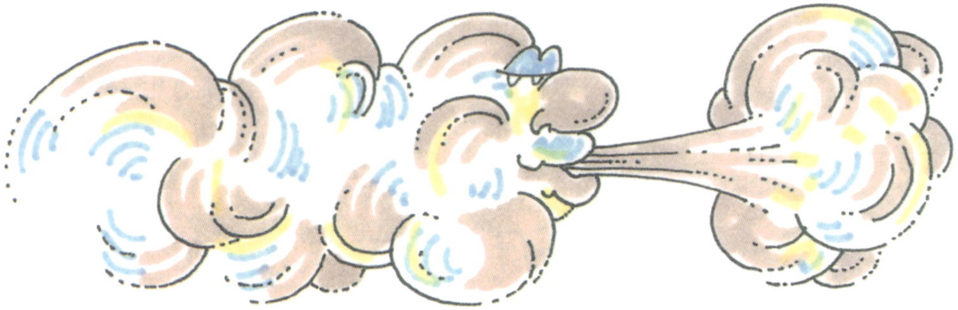

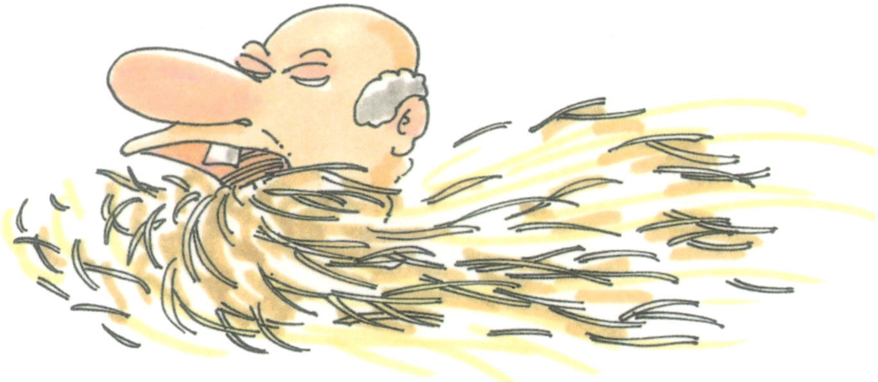

Two Bar Eighth Note Strum Patterns

On page 9, you were introduced to two-bar strum patterns. The two-bar strum pattern written below contains eighth note strums in the first bar (Strum Pattern Number Four), and half note strums in the second bar. Practice this new two-bar strum holding a C chord. When you are confident playing it, apply it to the song **Shortnin' Bread**.

Bar 1	Bar 2
V ∧ V ∧ V V	V V
Count: 1 + 2 + 3 4	1 2 3 4

17 Shortnin' Bread

Bars **4** and **8** each contain two chords. Change to the second chord on the **third** beat of the bar. Also, in bars **4** and **8**, to play the rest you must lightly touch the open third string with the **second** finger of your left hand, to stop it from sounding.

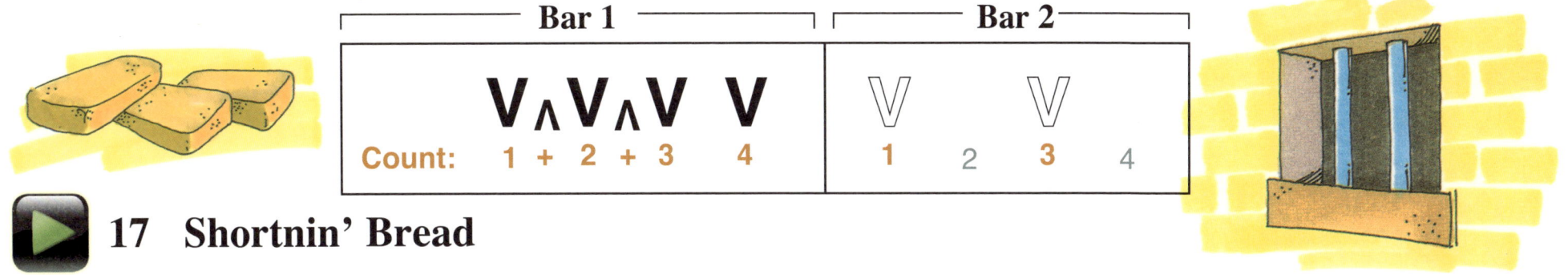

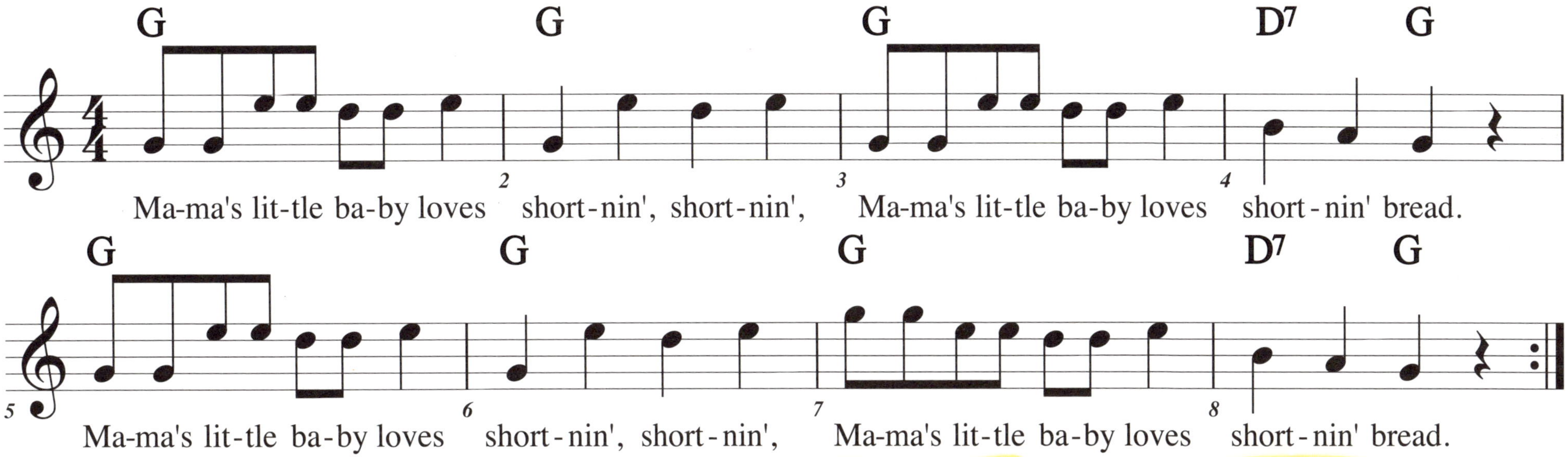

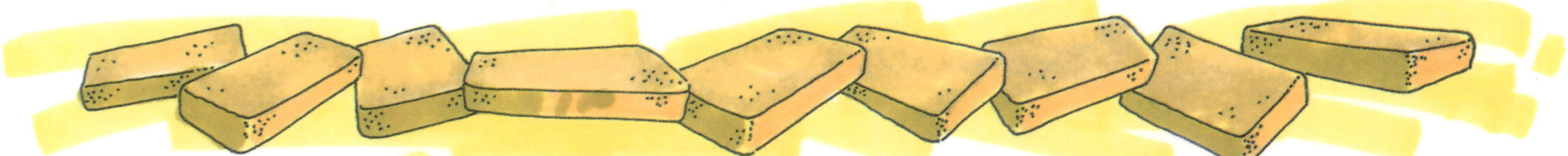

You can now play the songs on pages 14 to 17 of Guitar Method for Young Beginners, Supplementary Songbook A.

Lesson 6

 **The Dotted Quarter Note**

A dot written after a quarter note means that you hold the note for **one and a half** counts. A **dotted quarter note** is sometimes called a dotted crotchet and is often followed by an eighth note.

18

1 2 + 3 4

19 Quarter Dot Rock

Strum Pattern: V ⌄ V ⌄ V V
1 + 2 + 3 4

G   D⁷   D⁷   G

20 The Muffin Man

Strum Pattern: V   V
1 2 3 4

C   C   D⁷   G
Do you know the Muf-fin man, the Muf-fin man, the Muf-fin man?

C   C   G⁷   C
Do you know the Muf-fin man, his wares are such a treat?

Lesson 7

First and Second Endings

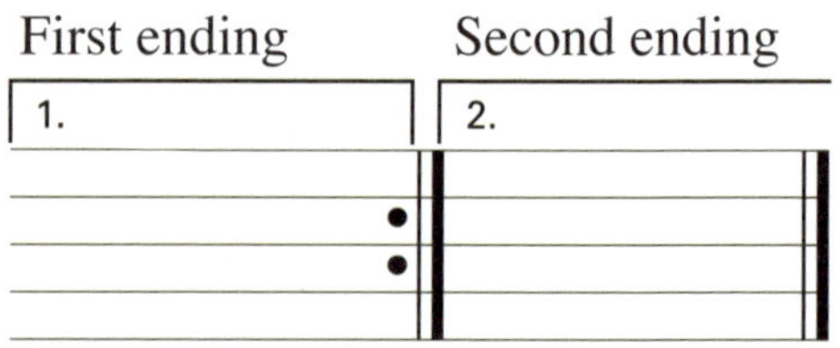

The next two songs contain **first and second endings**. The first time you play through the song, play the first ending (1.), then go back to the beginning. The **second** time you play through the song, play the second ending (2.) instead of the first.

 **22   Home, Sweet Home**

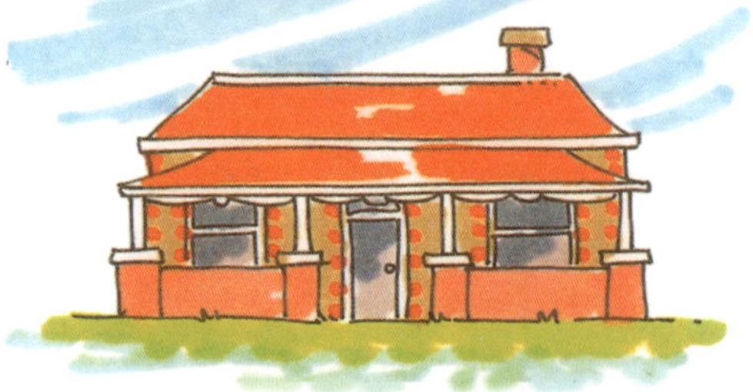

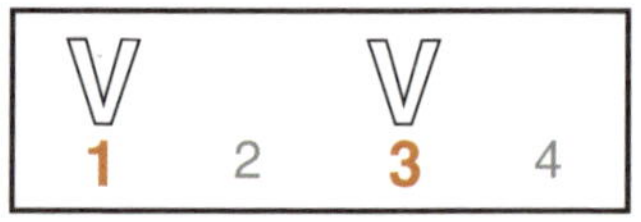

In this song, play through to the end of the **first** ending (bar **4**), then repeat the song from the beginning, as indicated by the repeat dots. When you play through the song the **second** time, do not play bar 4 (the first ending), but play bar **5** (the second ending) instead. The repeat dots at the end of bar 5 indicate that the whole song is repeated. On the recording there are **three** drumbeats to introduce this song.

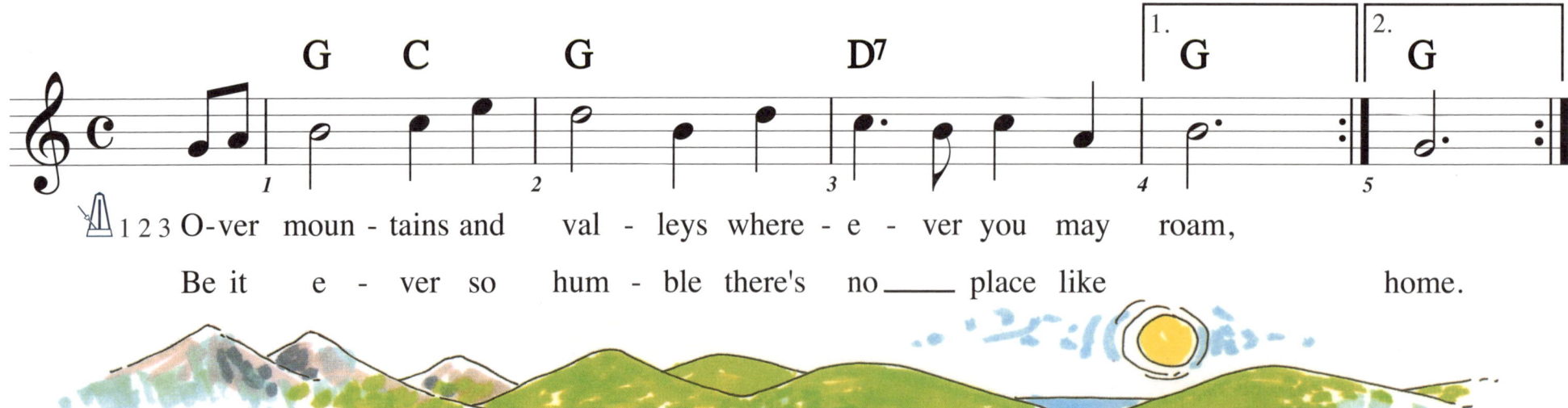

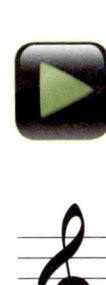

Strum Pattern

V V V
1 2 3 4

23 Jingle Bells

G G G G C
Jin - gle Bells, Jin - gle Bells, jin - gle all the way, O what fun it
G
1. D7 D7
2. D7 G
is to ride on a one horse o - pen sleigh, hey! one horse o - pen sleigh.

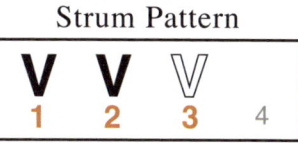

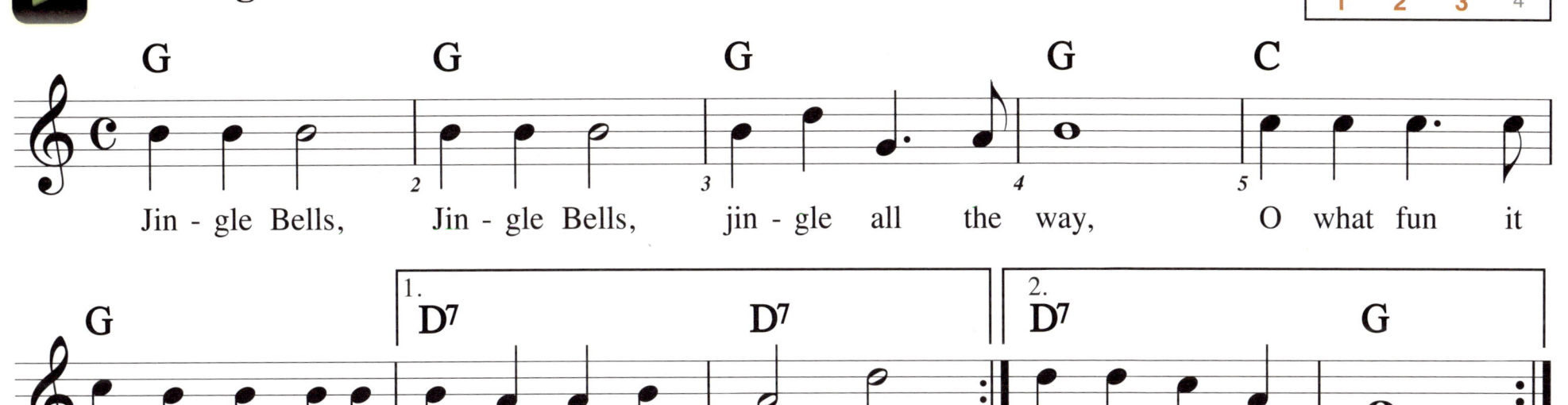

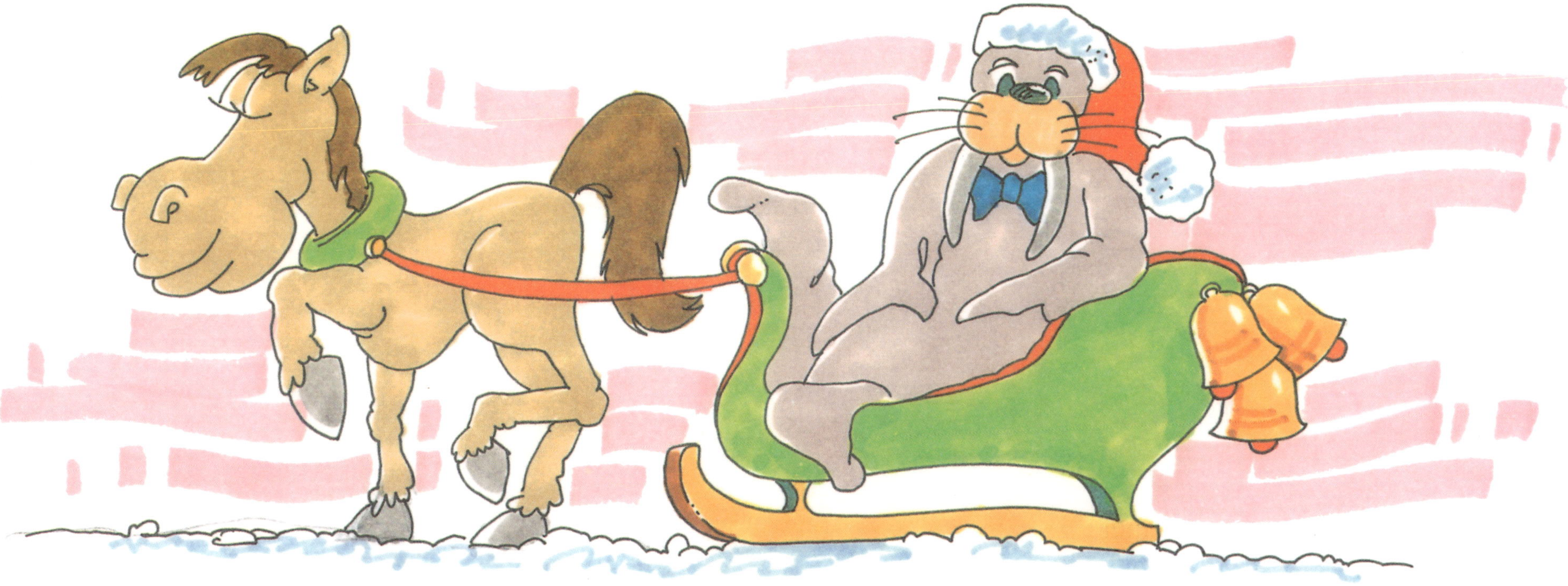

Lesson 8

The Open D Note

D Note

This is the **open D** note. It is written in the space below the staff.

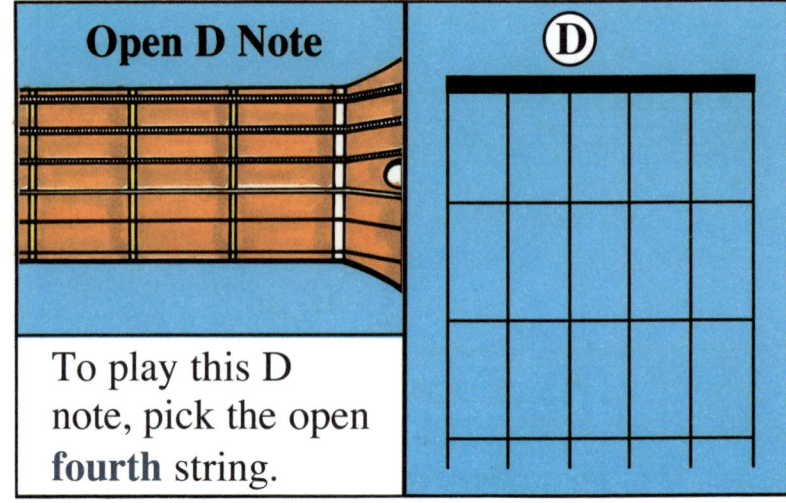

To play this D note, pick the open **fourth** string.

 **24 The Farmer in the Dell**

On the recording there are **five** drumbeats to introduce this song.

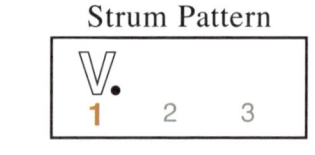

Strum Pattern

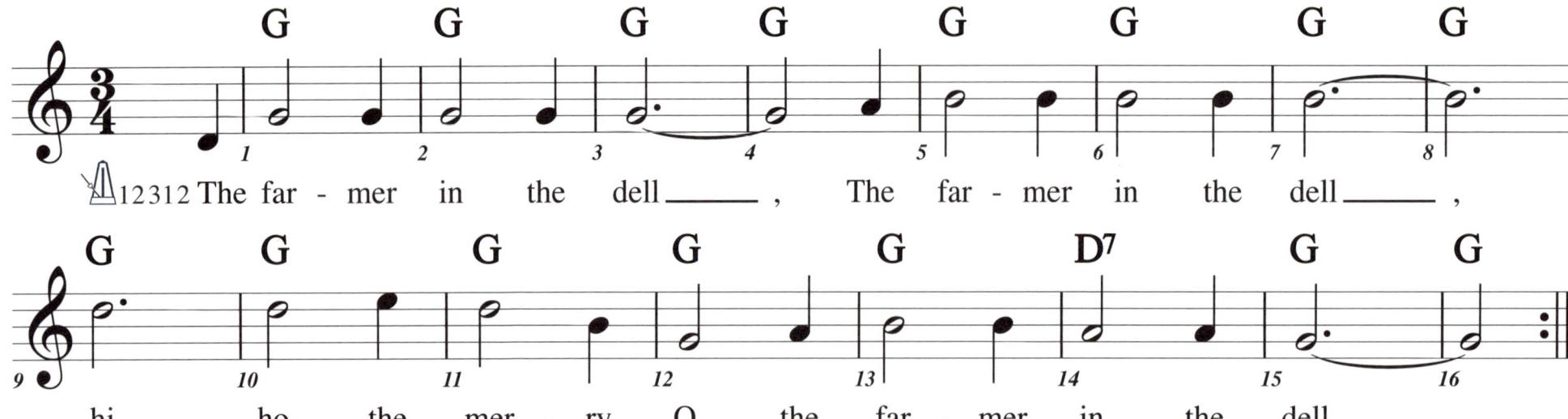

 **25 Brother John**

This song is a **round**. A round is a song where a second player can begin after the first has played a number of bars. In this song, the second player begins when the first player reaches bar **3**.

To make the chords of this song more interesting, different strums are written above the staff.

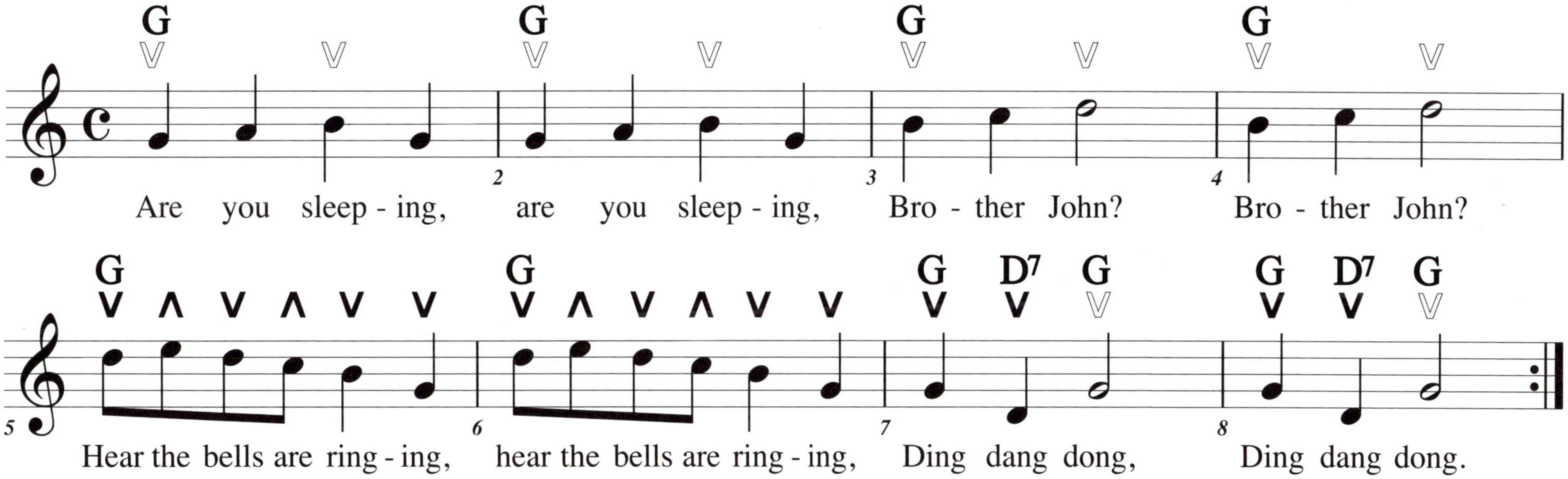

Are you sleep-ing, are you sleep-ing, Bro-ther John? Bro-ther John?

Hear the bells are ring-ing, hear the bells are ring-ing, Ding dang dong, Ding dang dong.

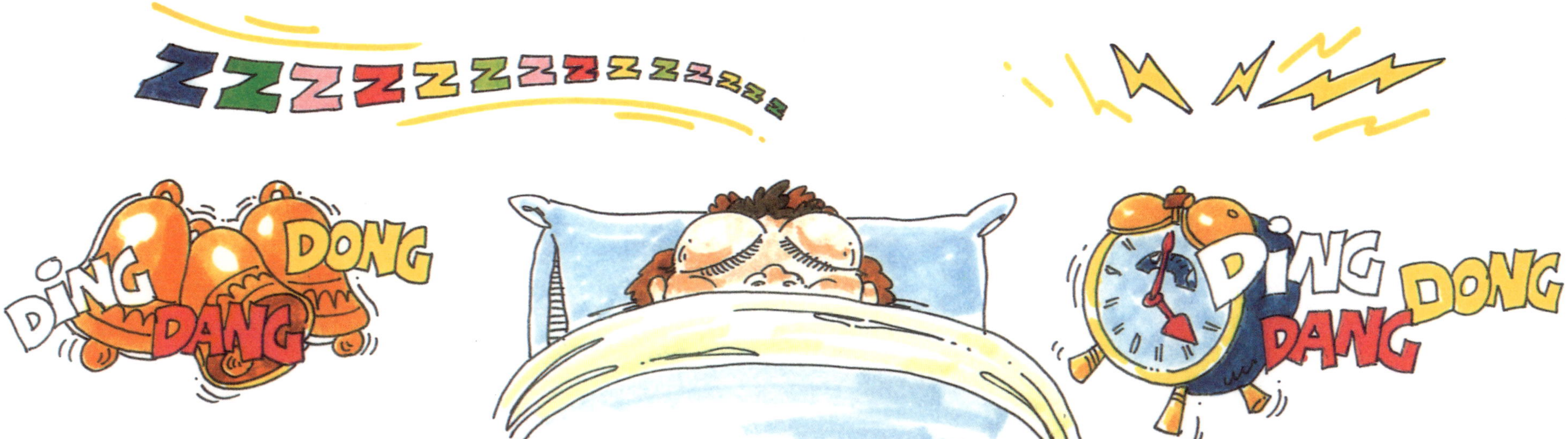

You can now play the songs on pages 22 to 24 of Guitar Method for Young Beginners, Supplementary Songbook A.

Lesson 9

The D Chord

To play the **D** chord, use the **first**, **second** and **third** fingers of your left hand as shown in the diagram, but strum only **four** strings.

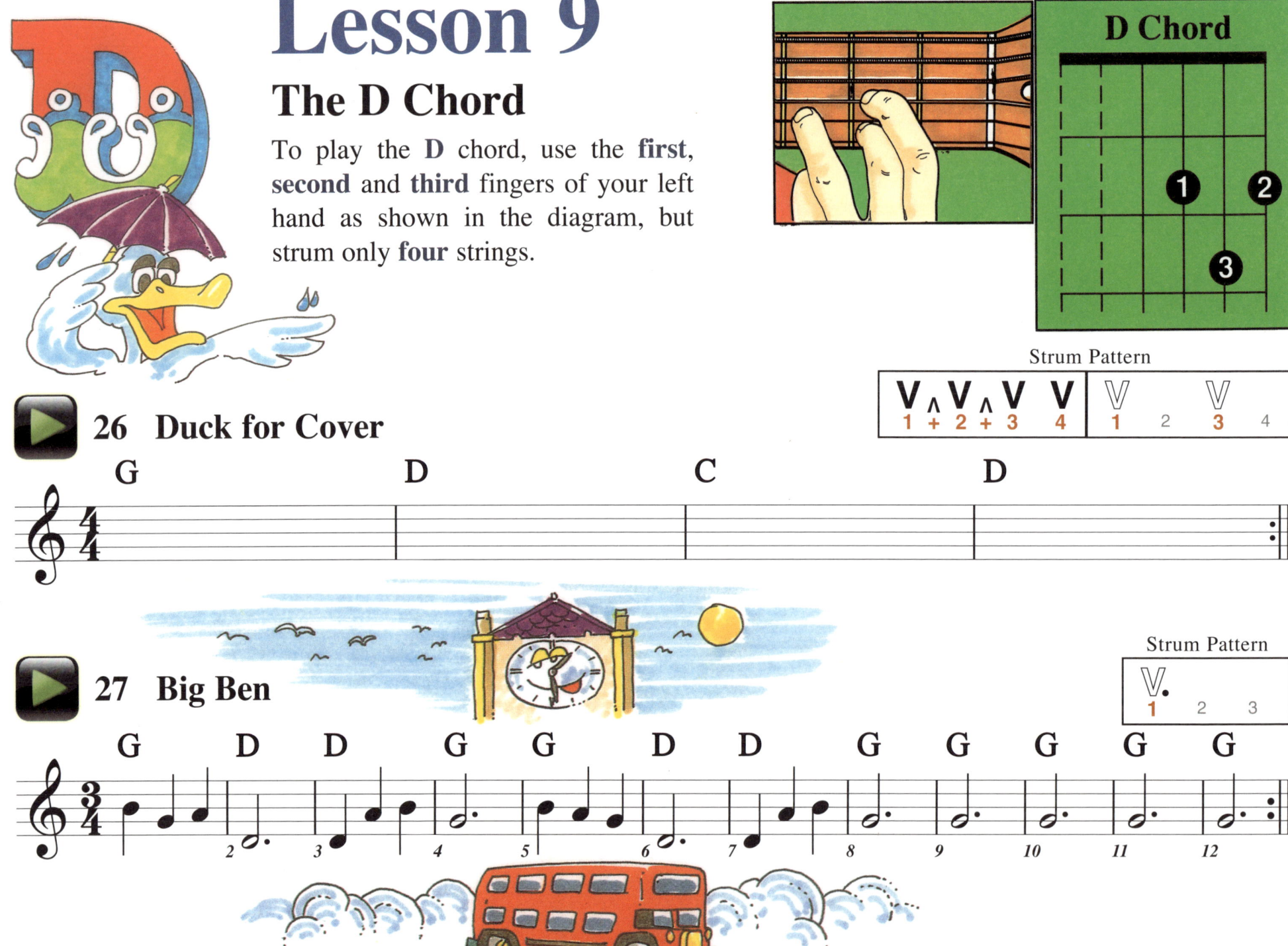

26 Duck for Cover

| G | D | C | D |

27 Big Ben

| G | D D | G G | D D | G G | G G | G G |

Eighth Note Strum Patterns in 3/4 time

On page 14 you were introduced to eighth note strum patterns in 4/4 time. Eighth note strum patterns can also be played in 3/4 time. Practice the following strum pattern, holding a G chord, then apply them to the song **Here We Go Round the Mulberry Bush**.

3/4 | V V∧V | **Strum Pattern Number One**
1   2 + 3

28 Here We Go Round the Mulberry Bush

Lesson 10

The Note F Sharp (F♯)

This is a **sharp sign**.

F♯ Note

A sharp sign written before a note on the staff means that you play the note that is one fret higher than the note written. For example, the note written on the staff above is called F sharp (F♯), and is played on the **second** fret of the **first** string. When a sharp sign is written on the staff it is always **written before** a note.

To play the note F♯, place your **second** finger just behind the **second** fret of the **first** string.

Is the note F♯ on the same or different place on the staff as F? ....

29 Autumn's Theme

Instead of writing a sharp sign before every F♯ note on the staff, it is easier to write just **one sharp sign** after the treble clef. This means that **all** the F notes on the staff are played as **F♯**, even though there is no sharp sign placed before them.

30 The Caissons Go Rolling Along

On the recording there are **six** drumbeats to introduce this song.

You can now play the songs on pages 25 to 28 of Guitar Method for Young Beginners, Supplementary Songbook A.

Notes and Rests

Name	Eighth Note (quaver)	Quarter Note (crotchet)	Dotted Quarter Note (dotted crotchet)	Half Note (minim)	Dotted Half Note (dotted minim)	Whole Note (semibreve)
Note	♪	♩	♩.	𝅗𝅥	𝅗𝅥.	𝅝
Rest	𝄾	𝄽	𝄽.	𝄼	𝄼 𝄽	𝄻
Number of Counts	$\frac{1}{2}$	1	$1\frac{1}{2}$	2	3	4

Notes

Chords

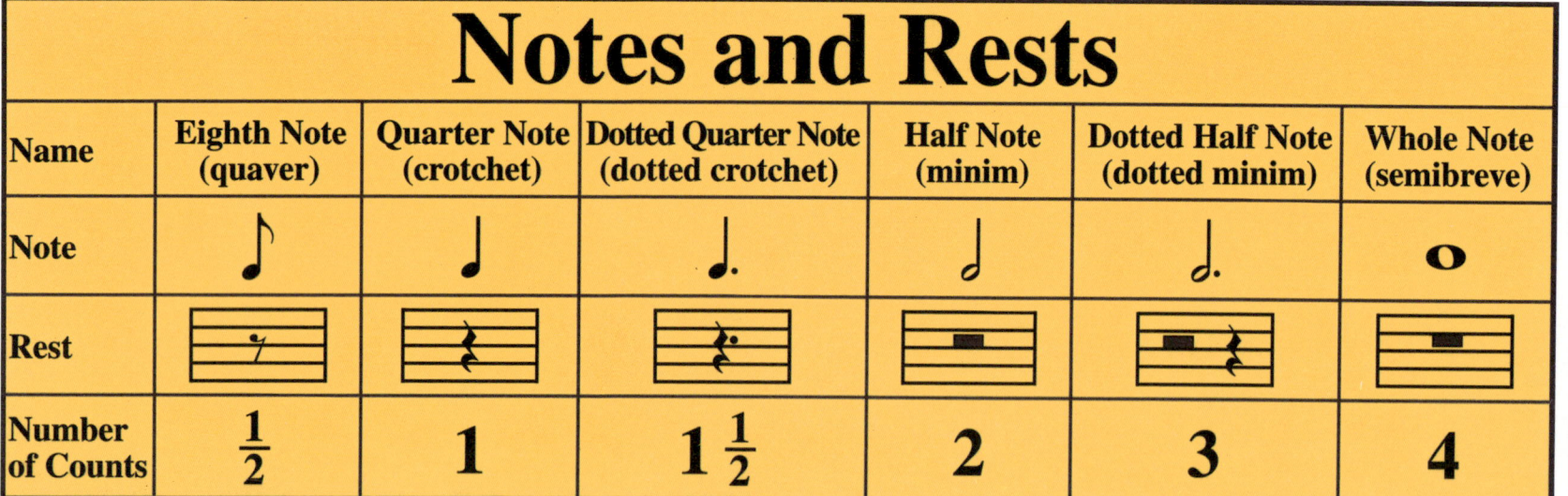

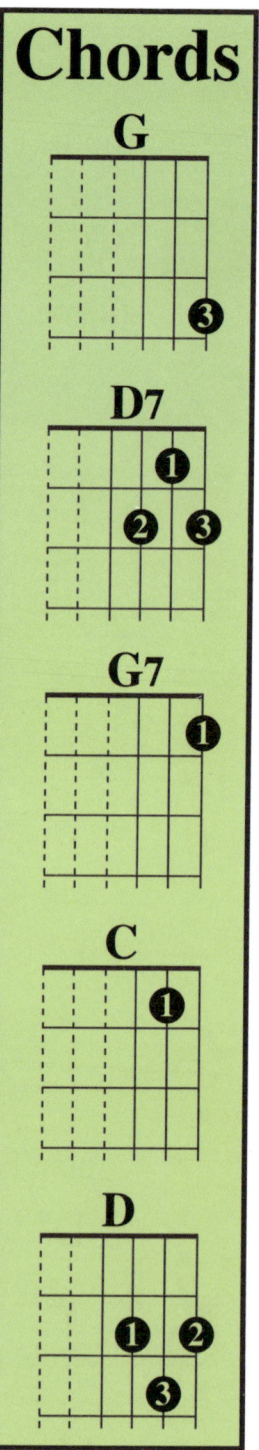

Congratulations on completing book 2. Now proceed to book 3.

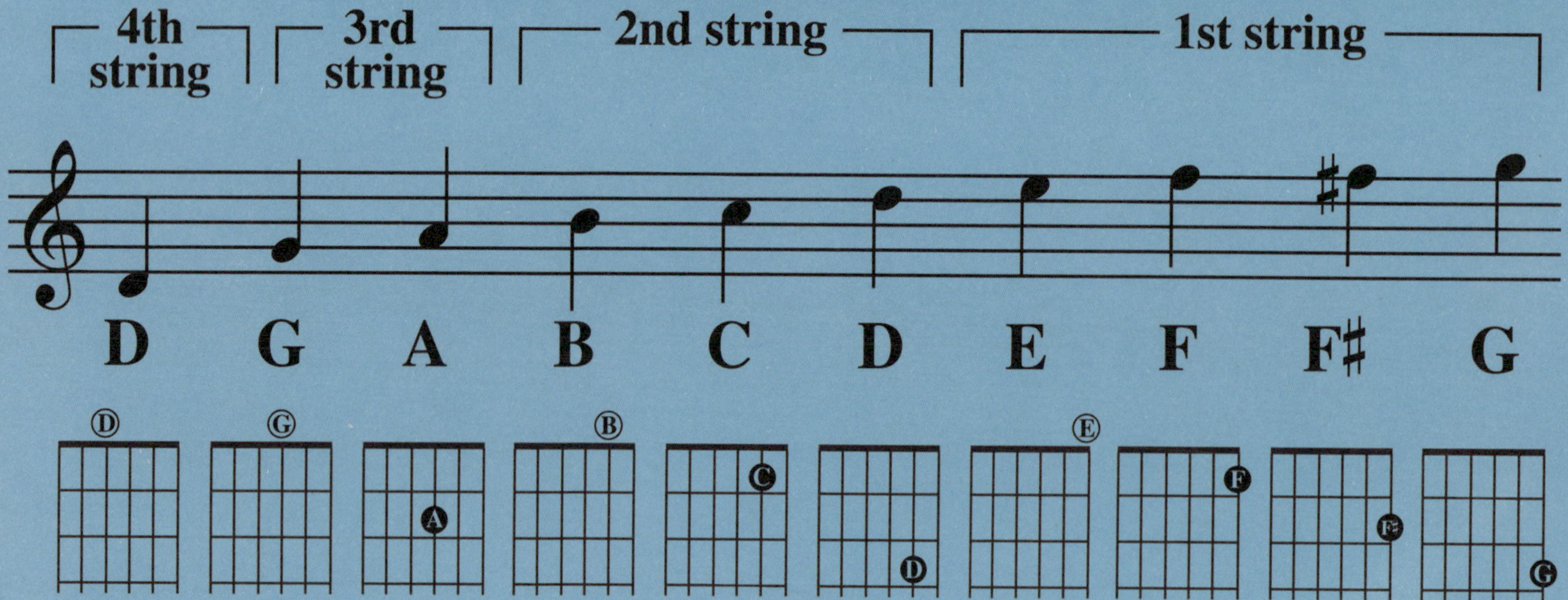